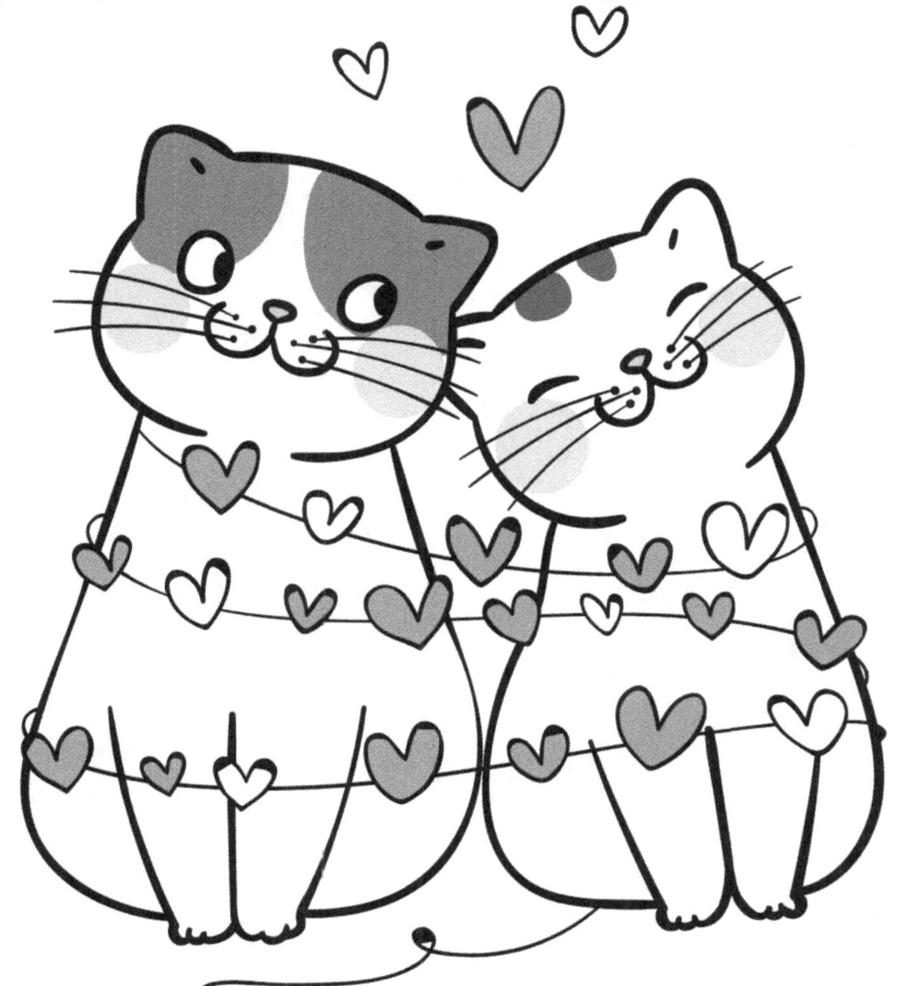

THIS BOOK BELONG TO

....

....

....

....

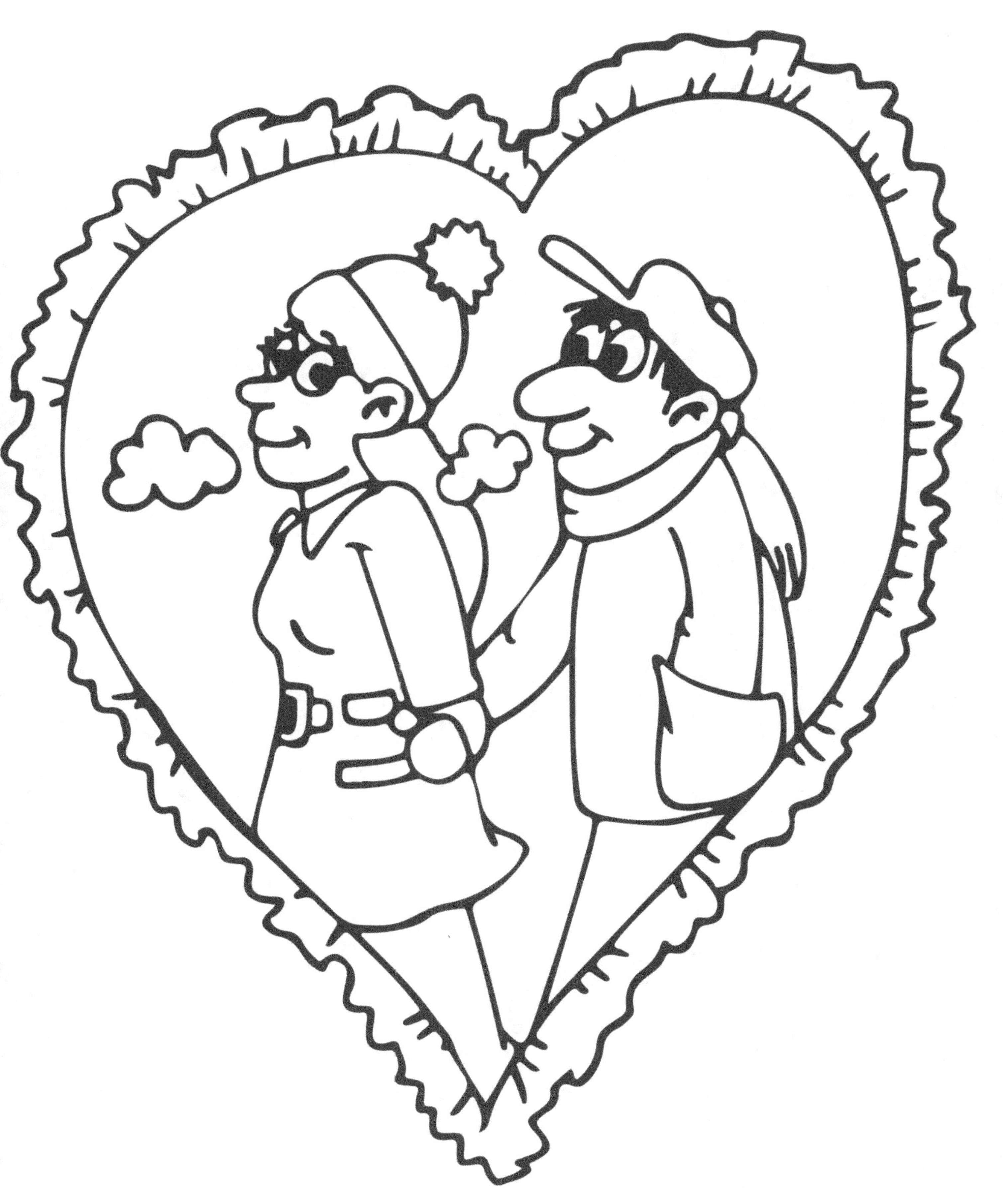

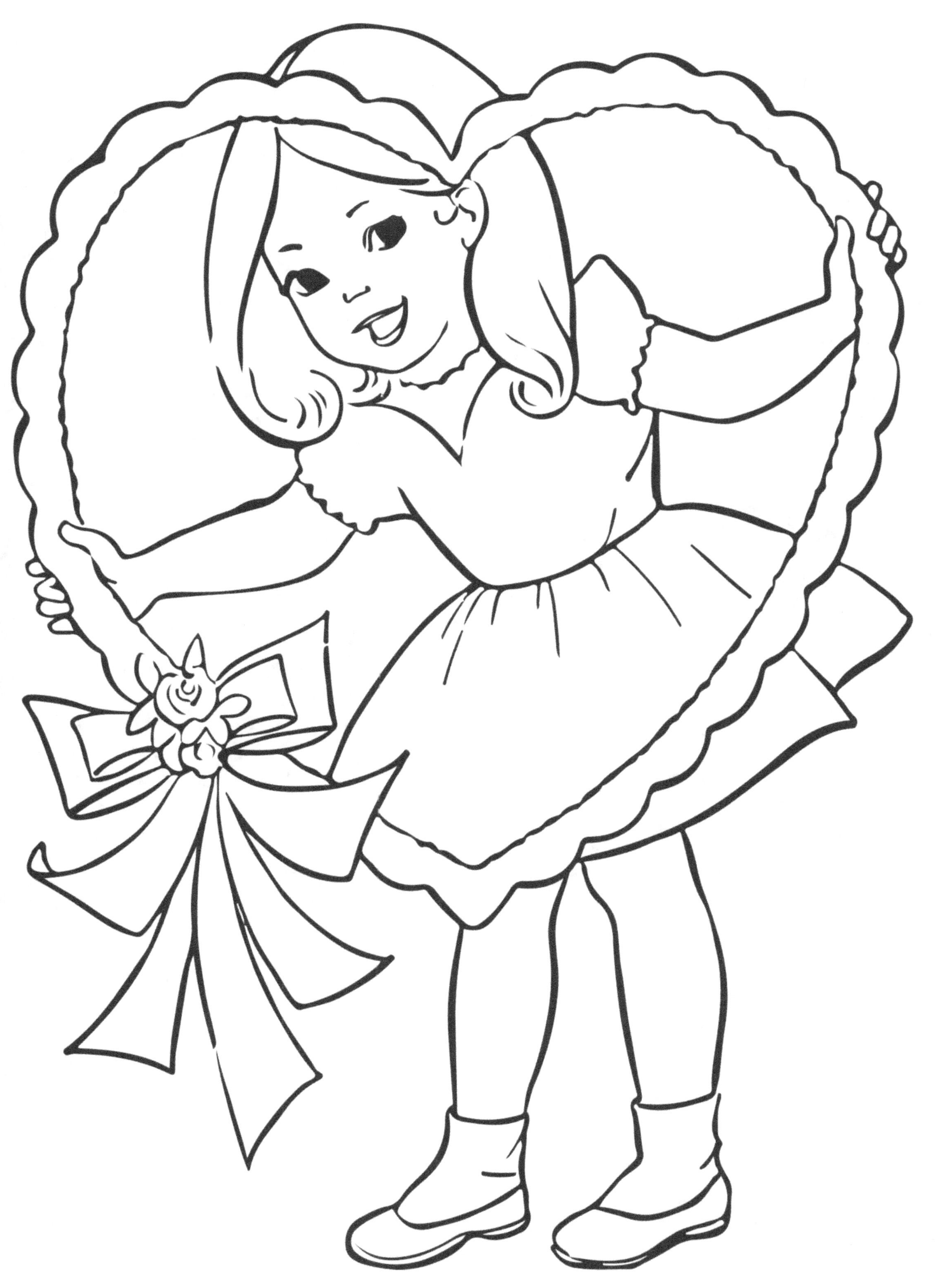

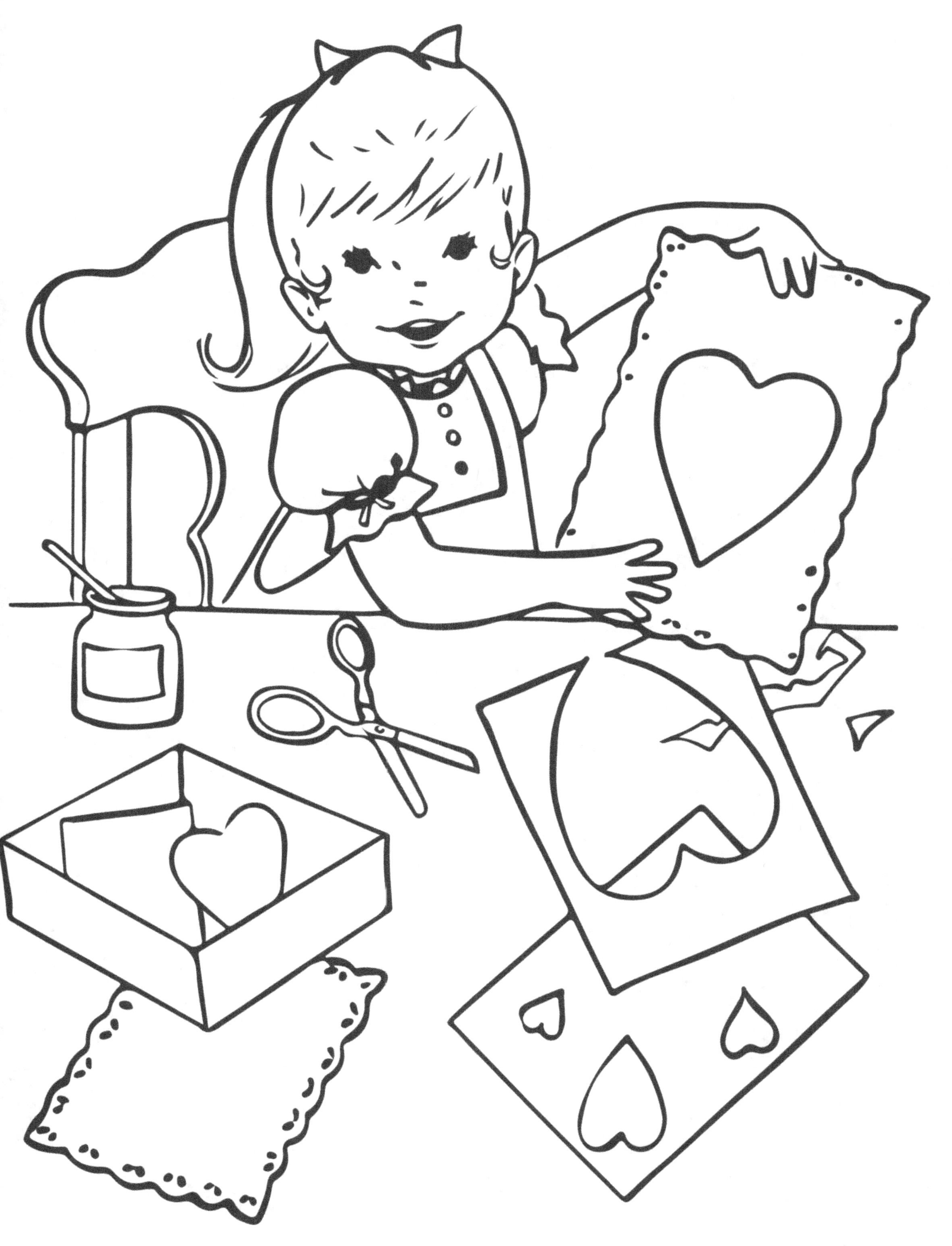

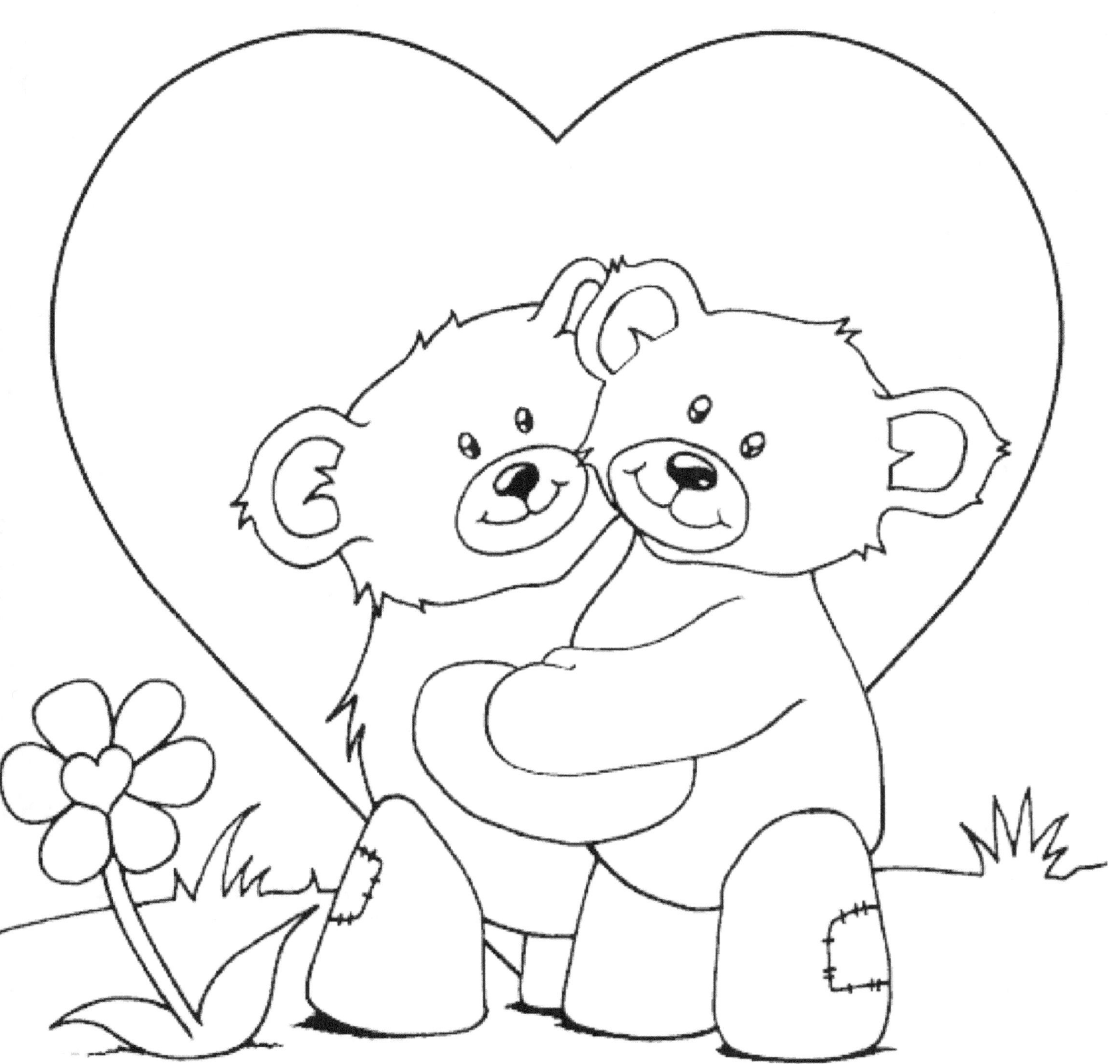

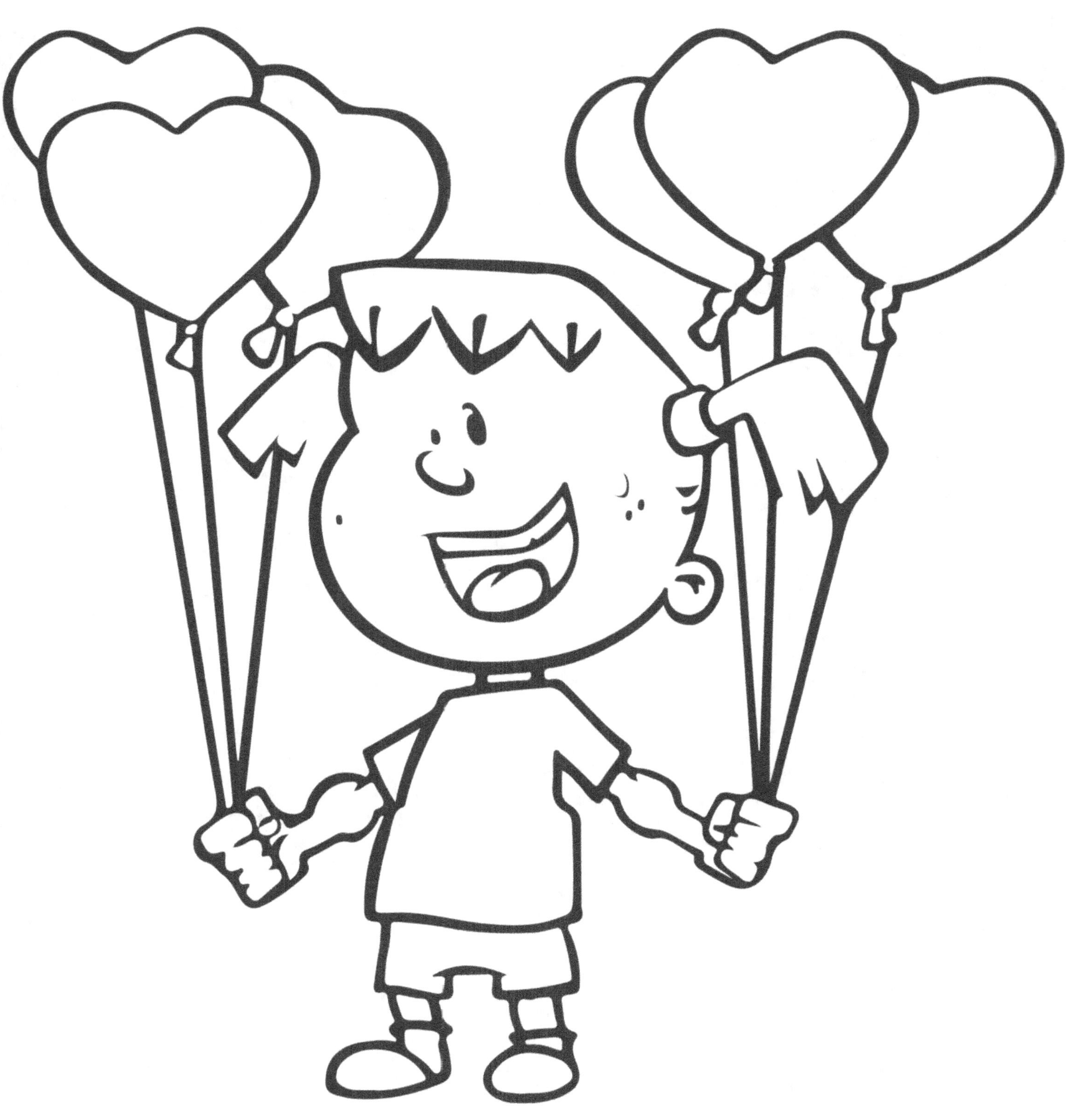

Happy
Valentine's Day

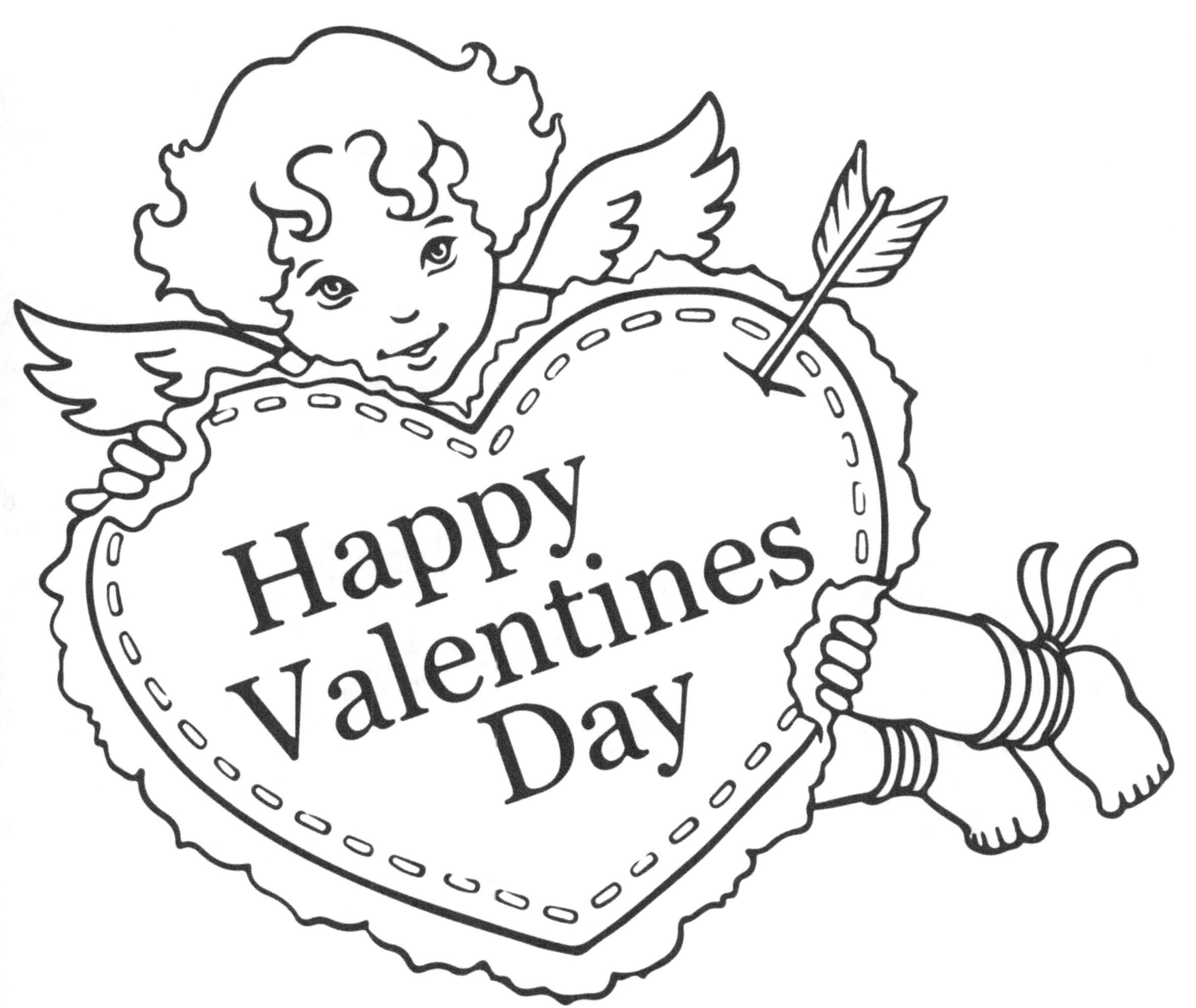
Happy
Valentines
Day

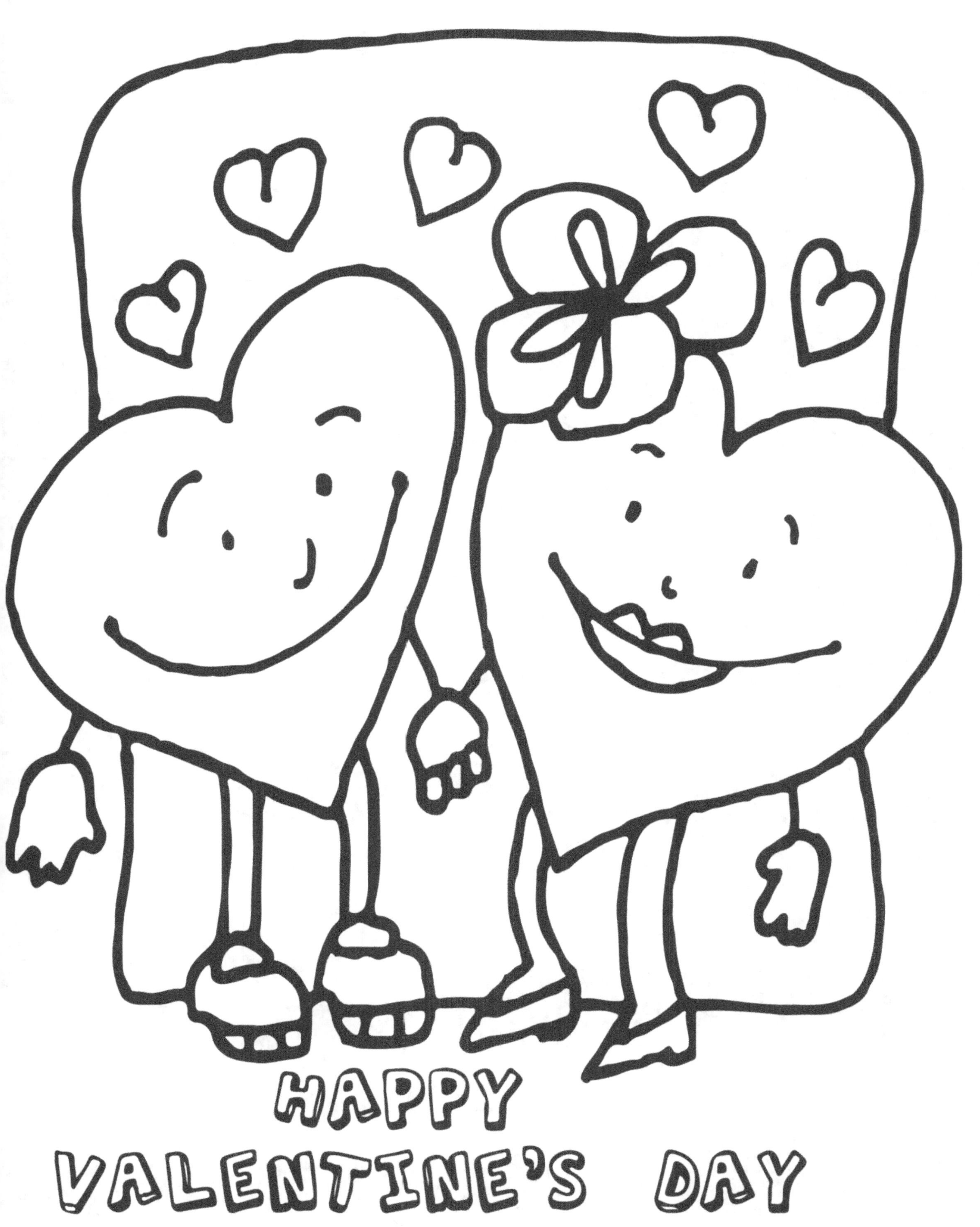

HAPPY
VALENTINE'S DAY

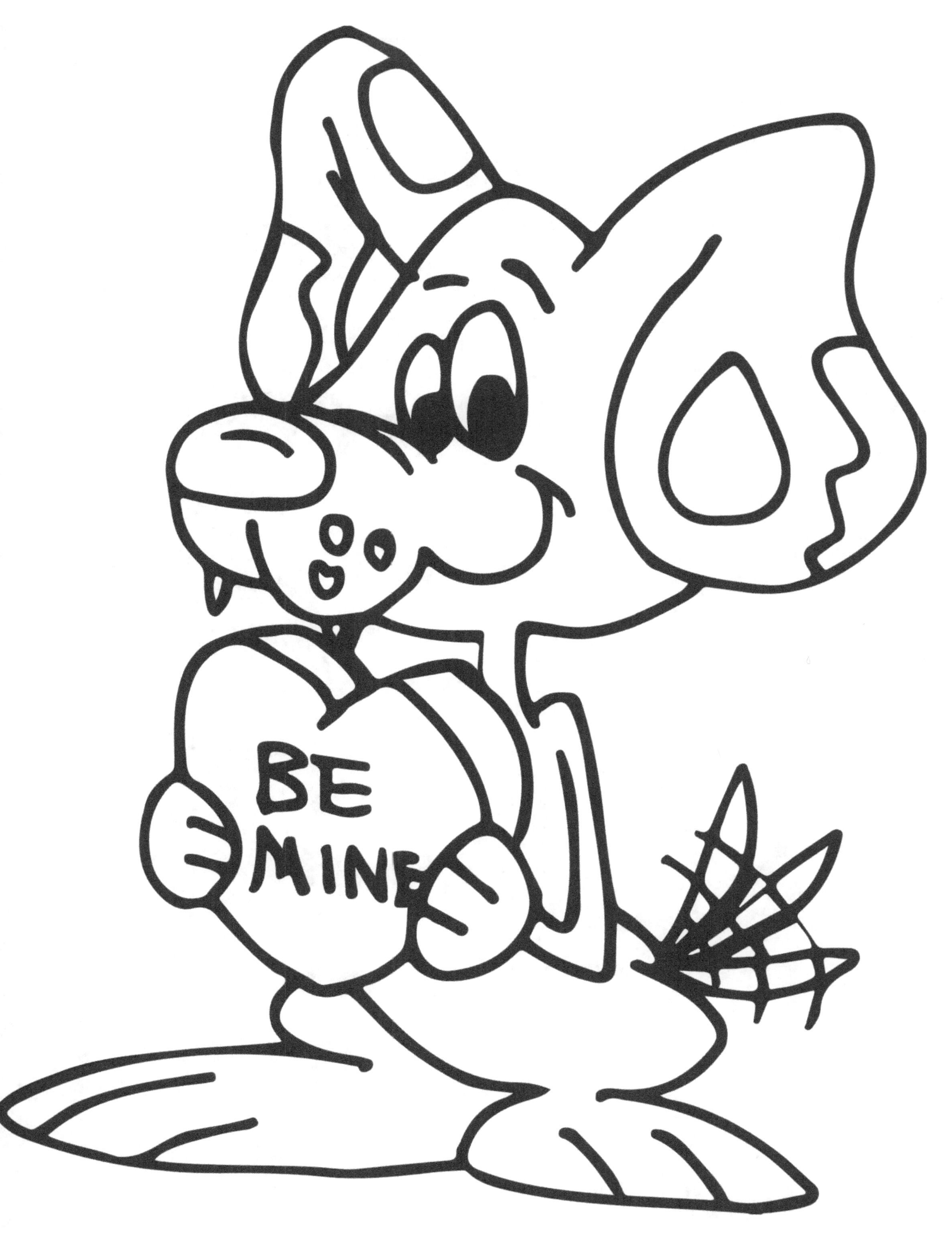
BE
MINE

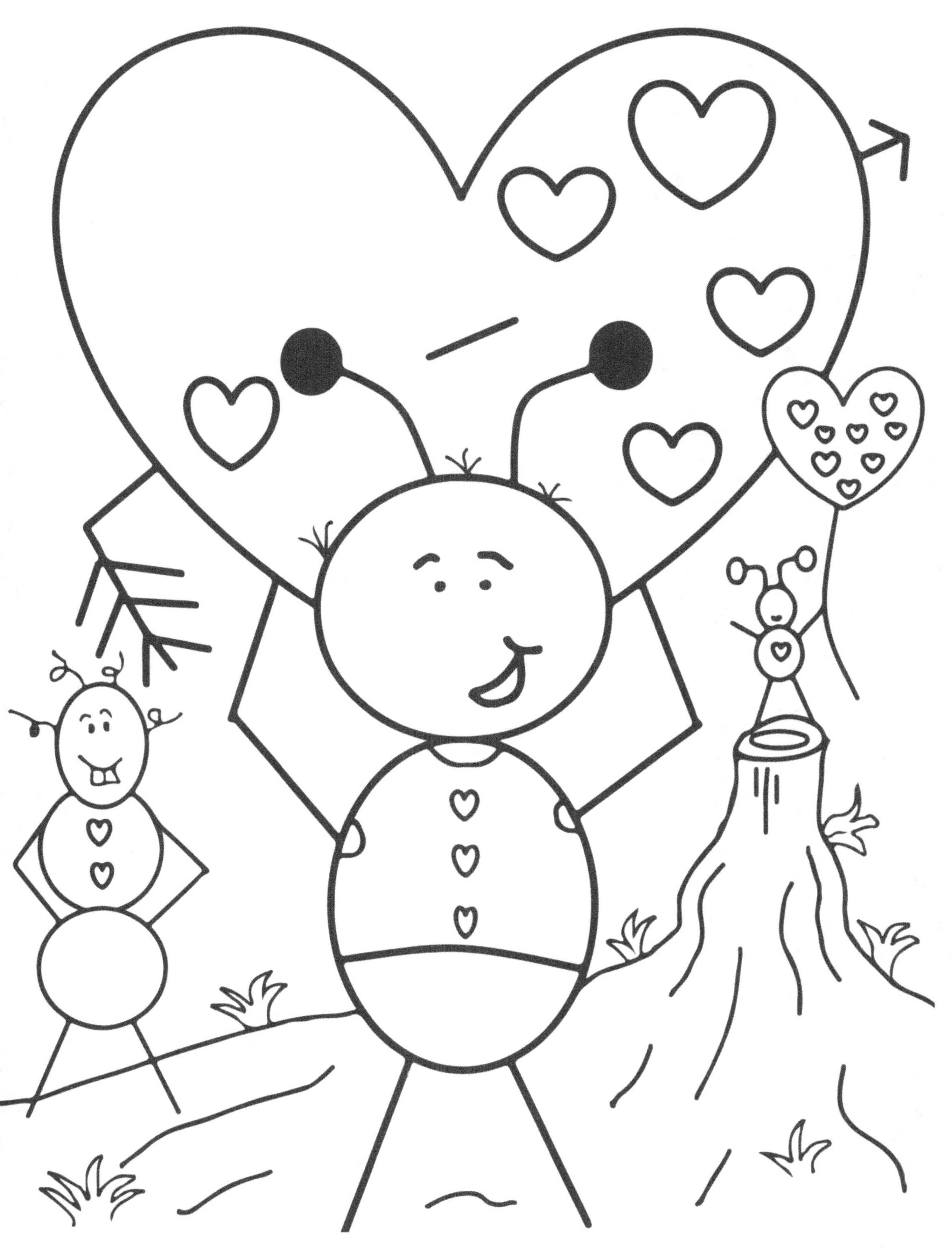

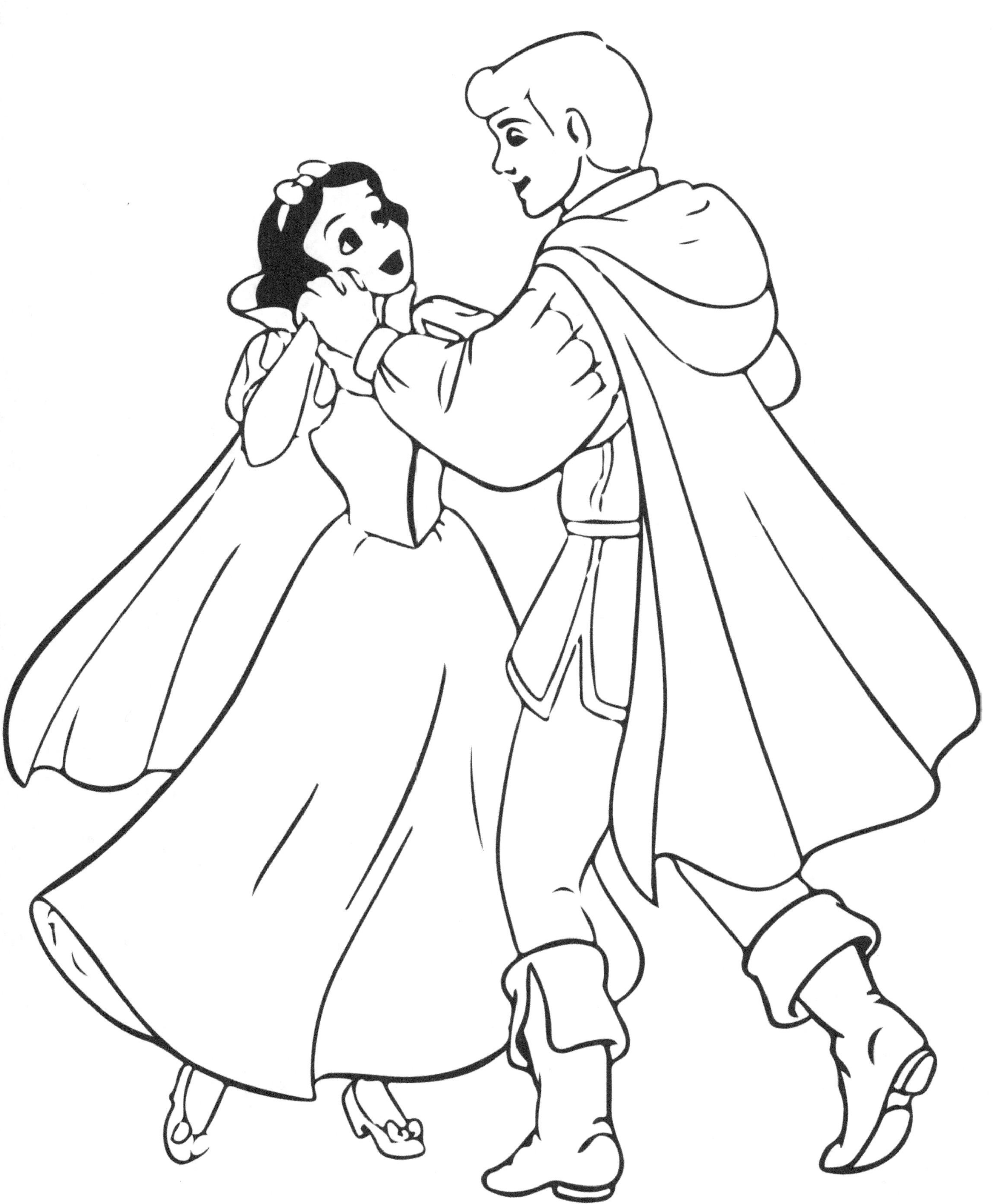

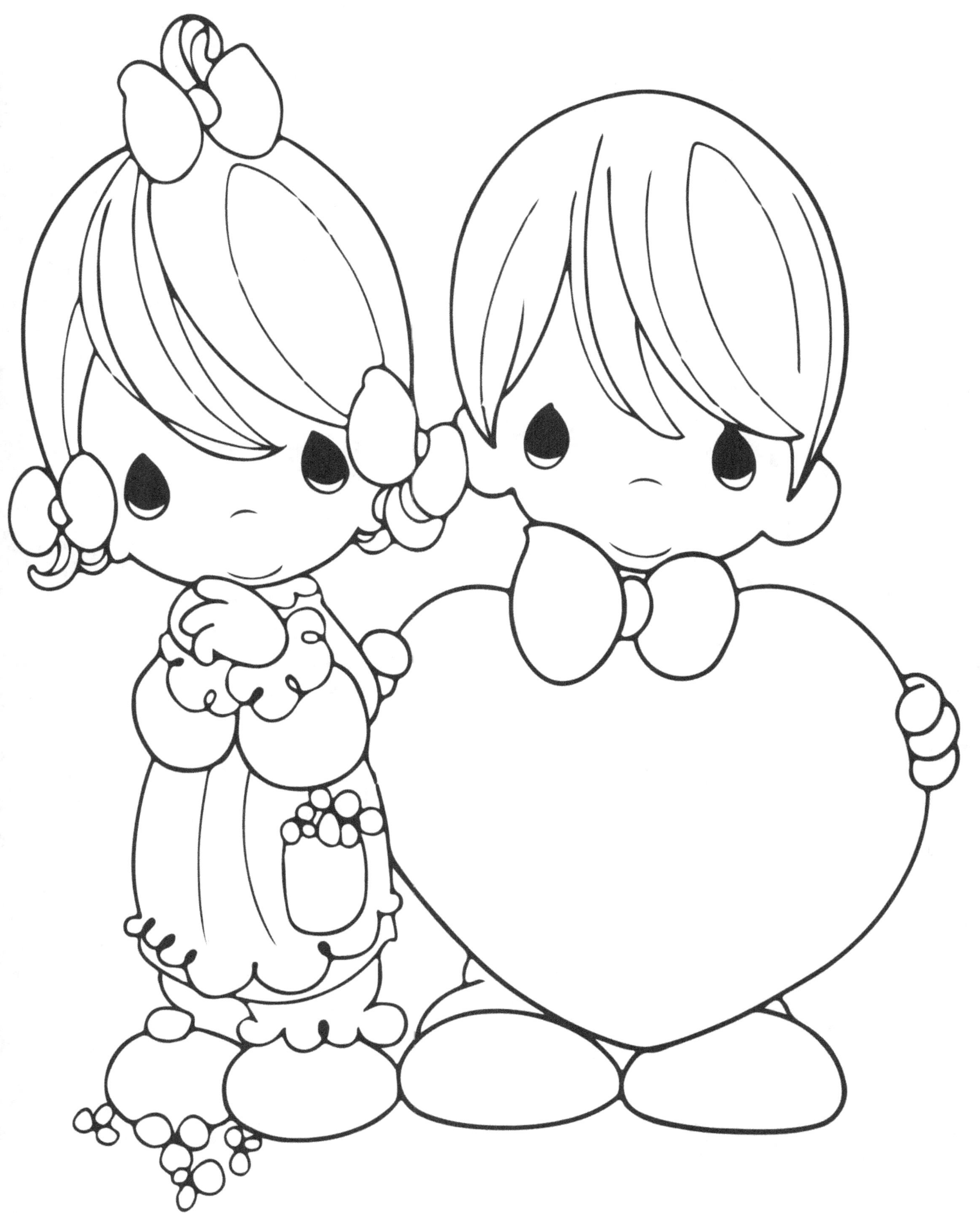

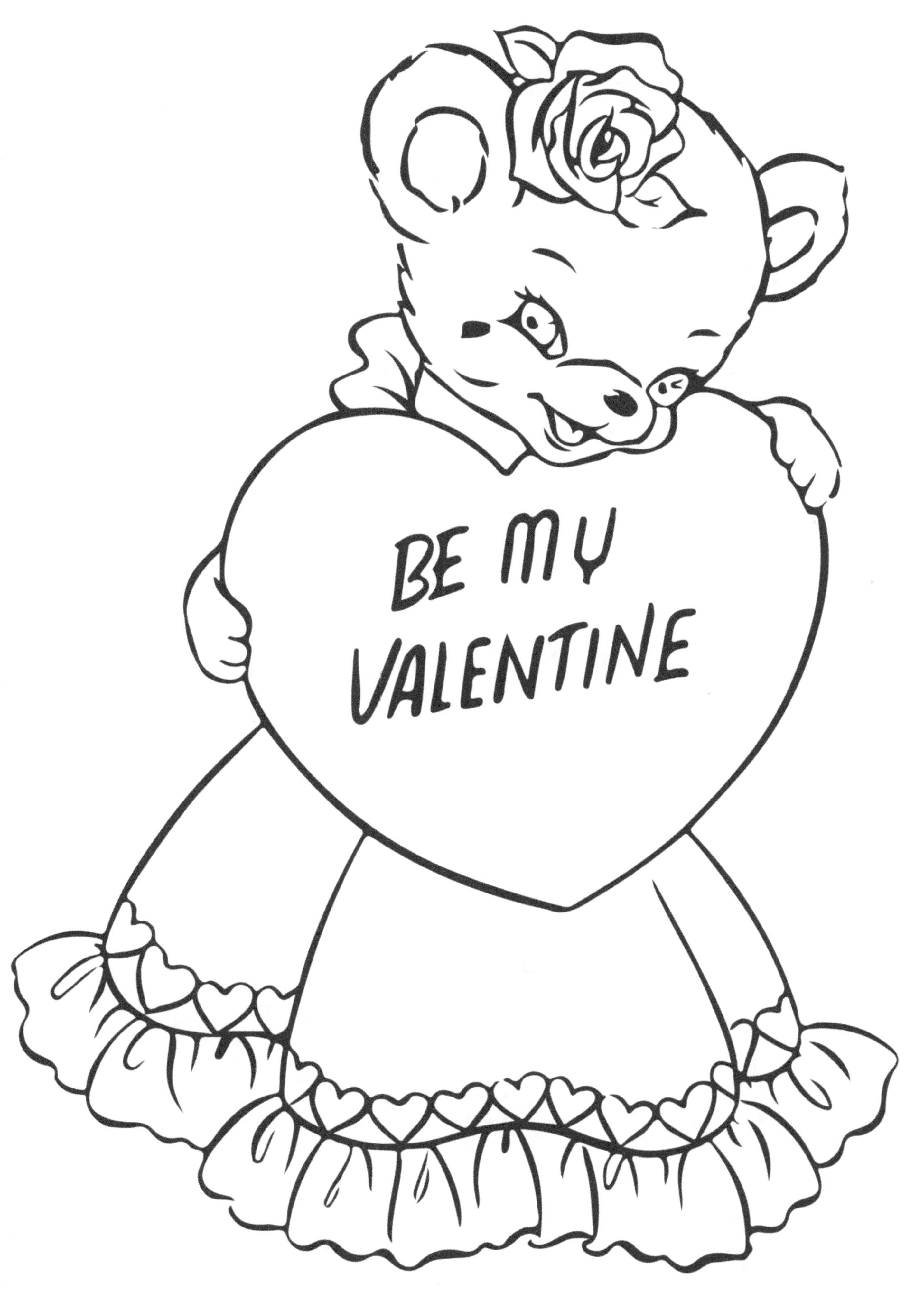

BE MY
VALENTINE

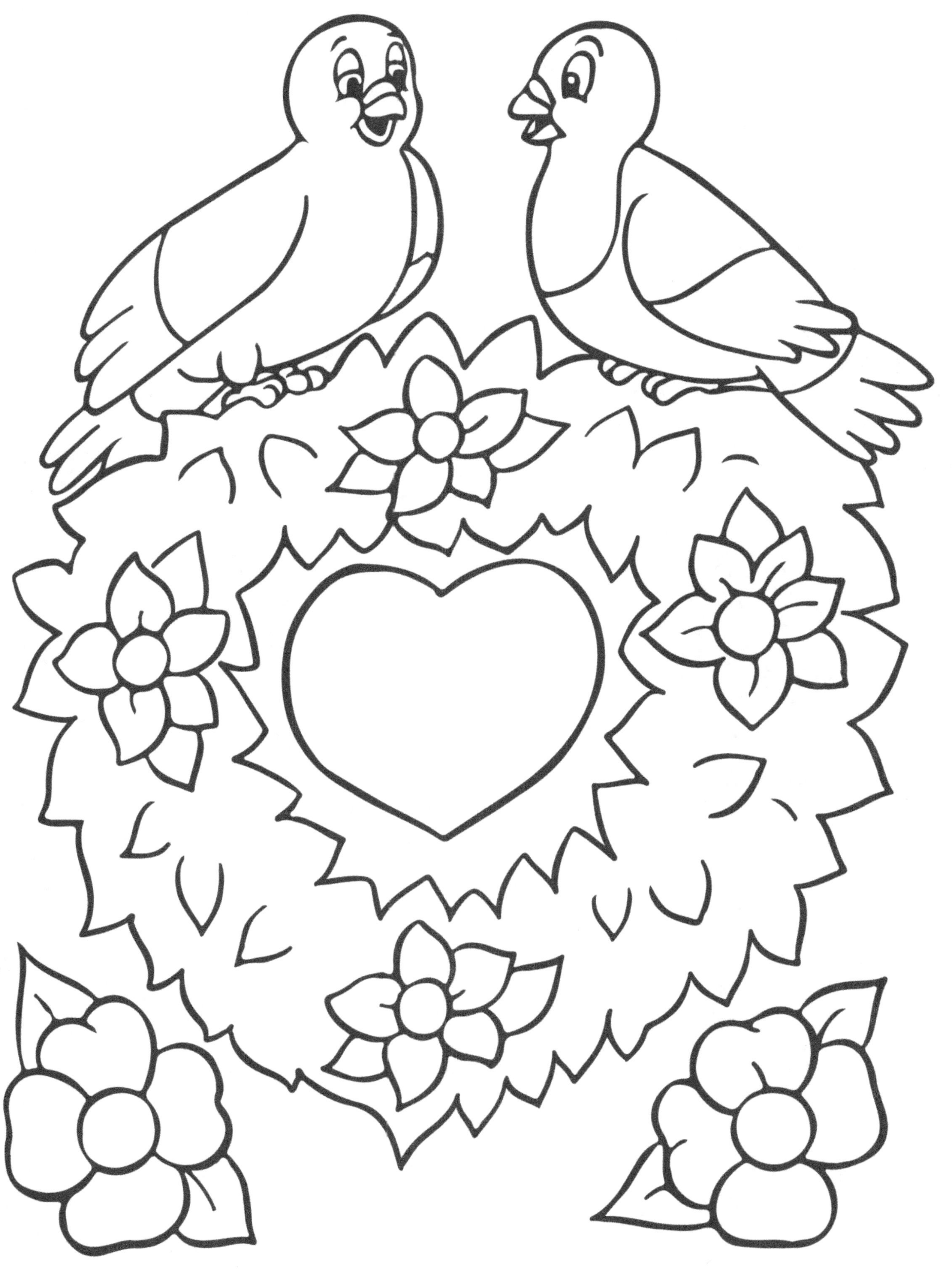

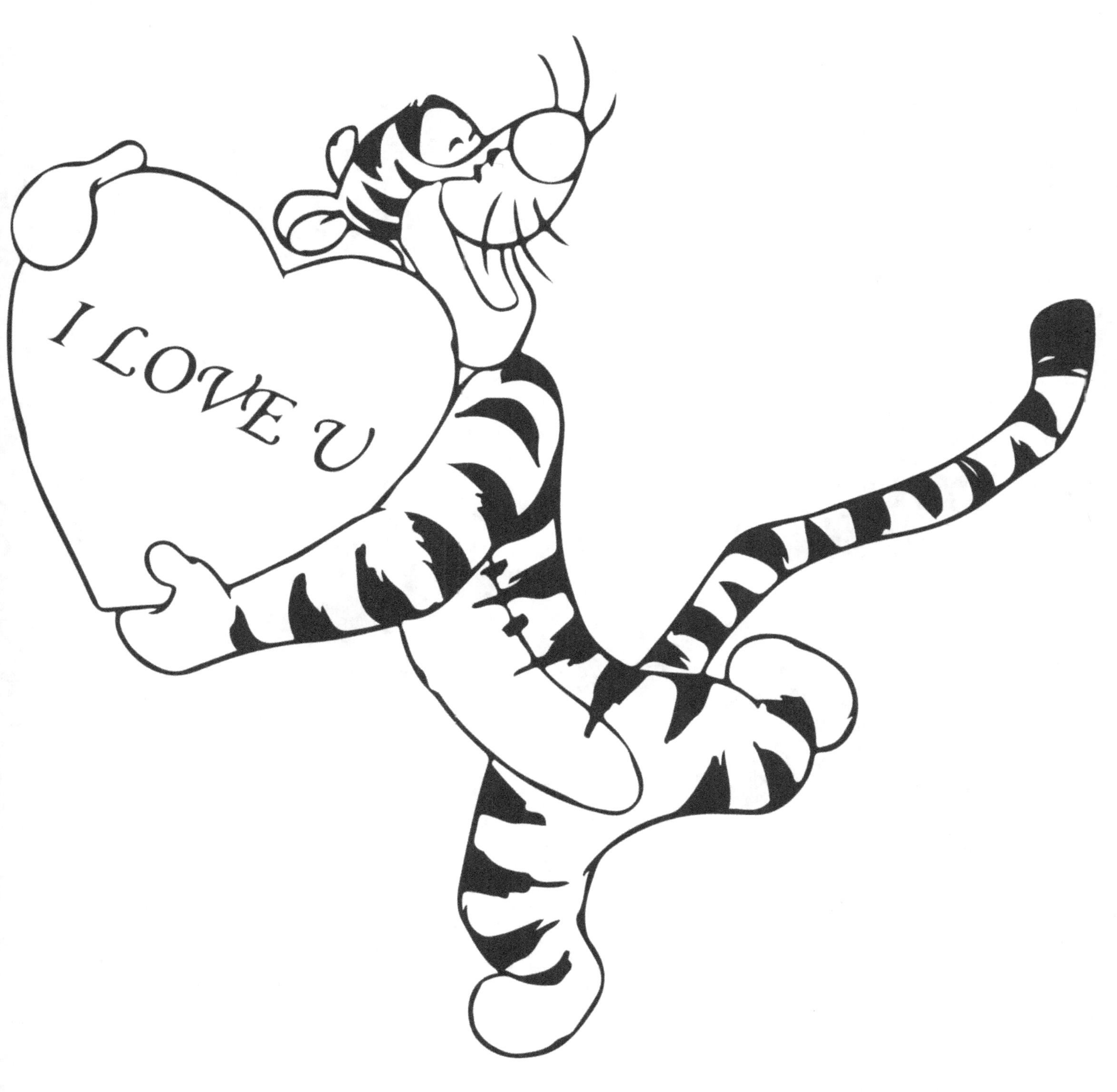
I LOVE U

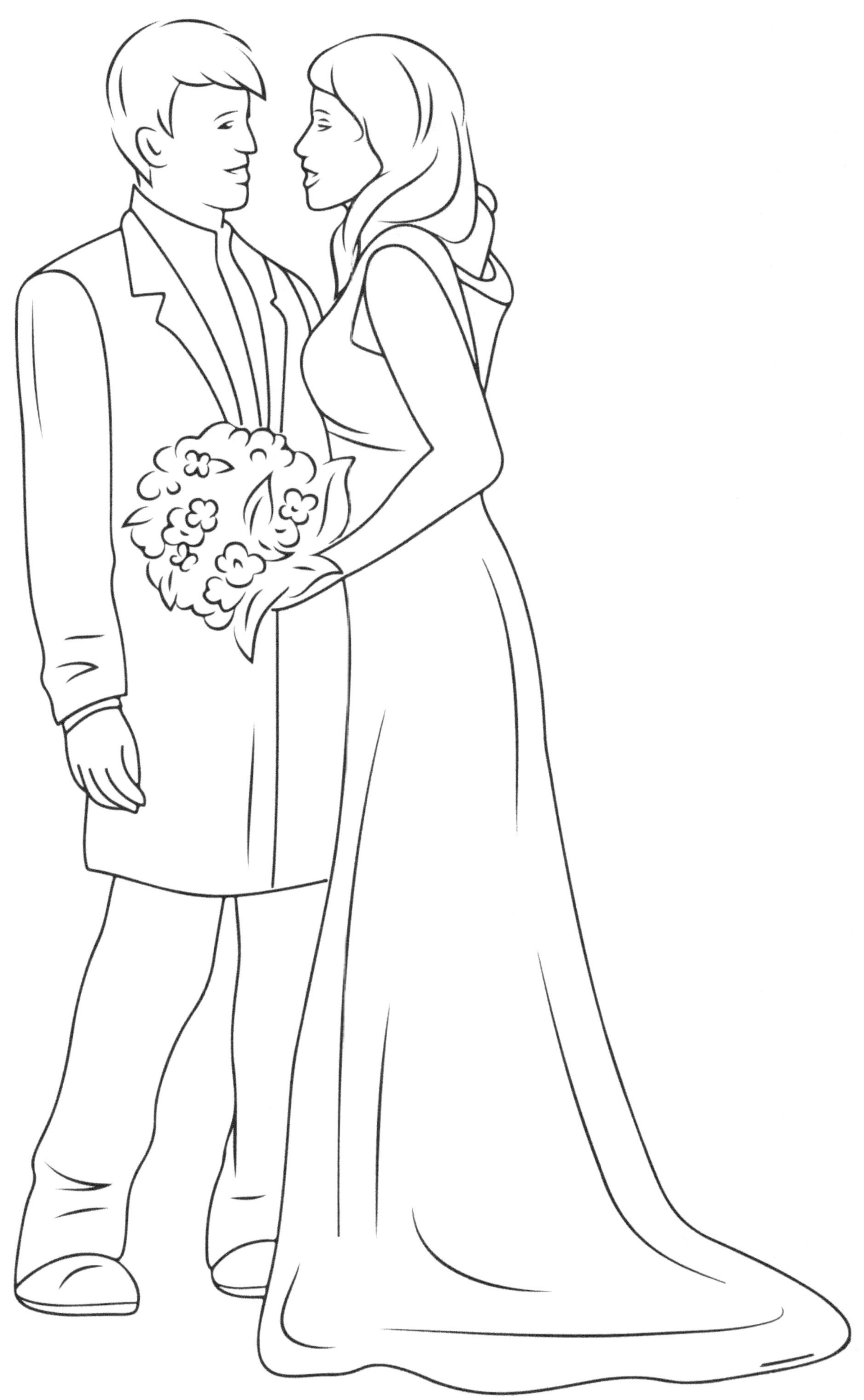

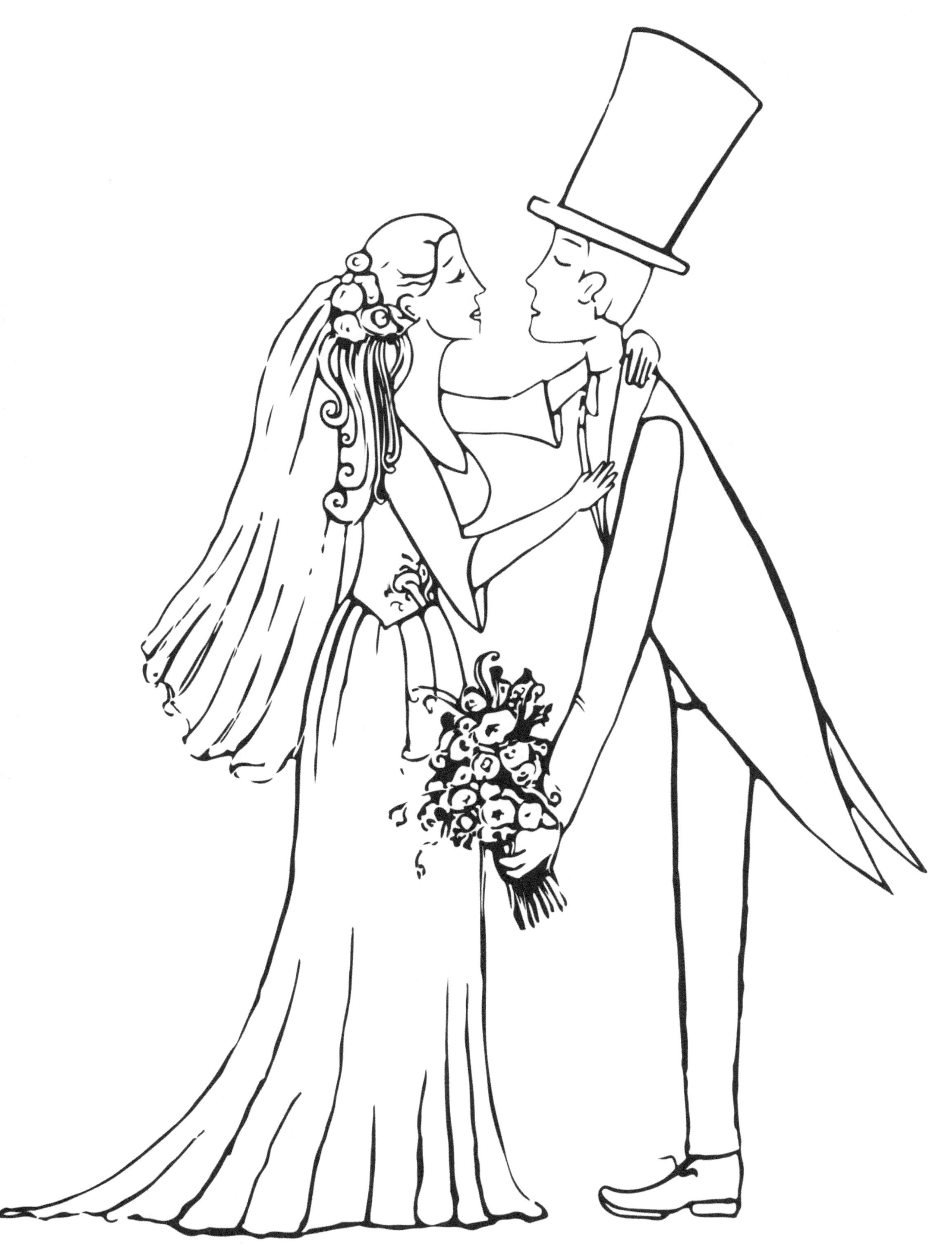

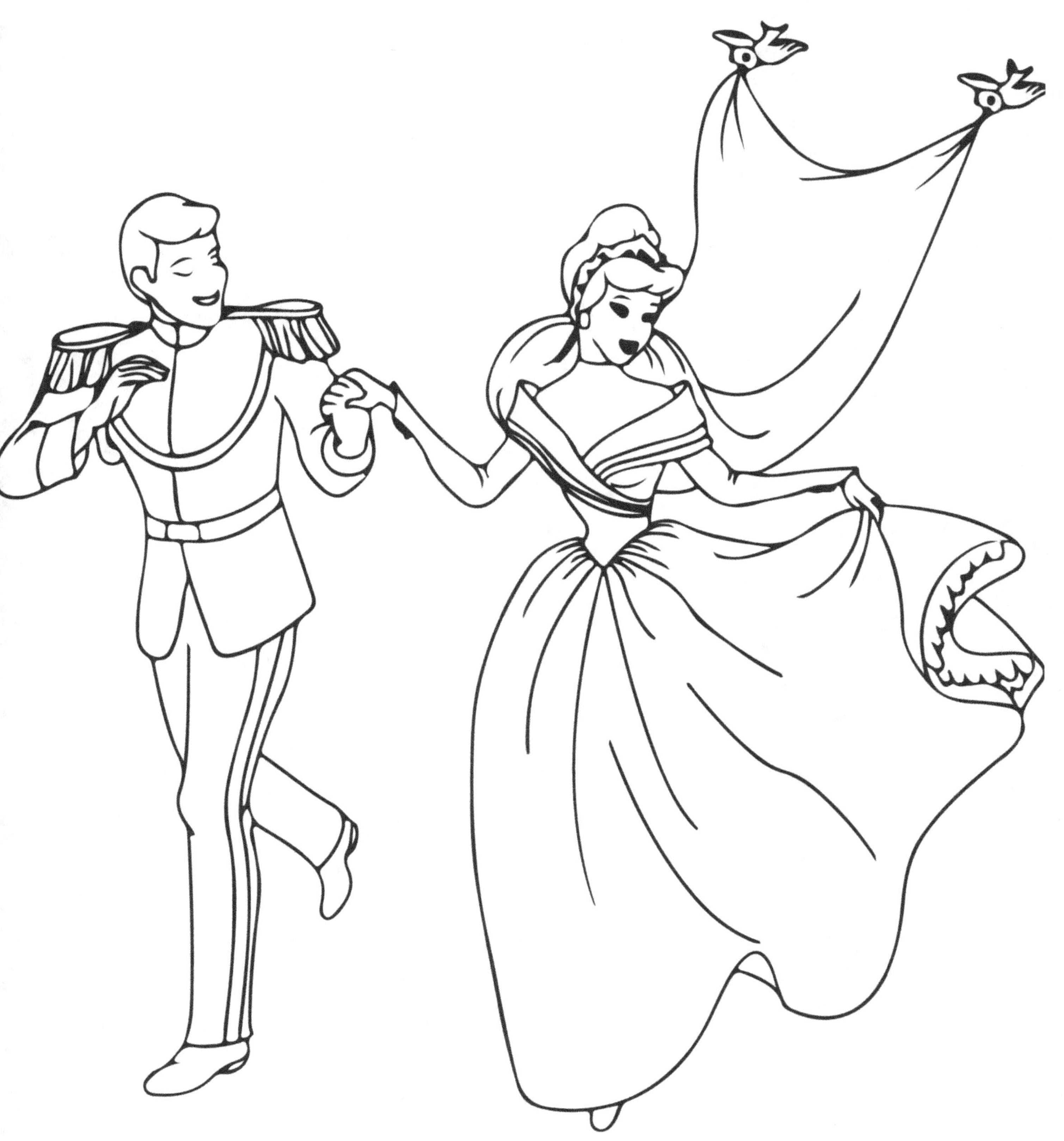

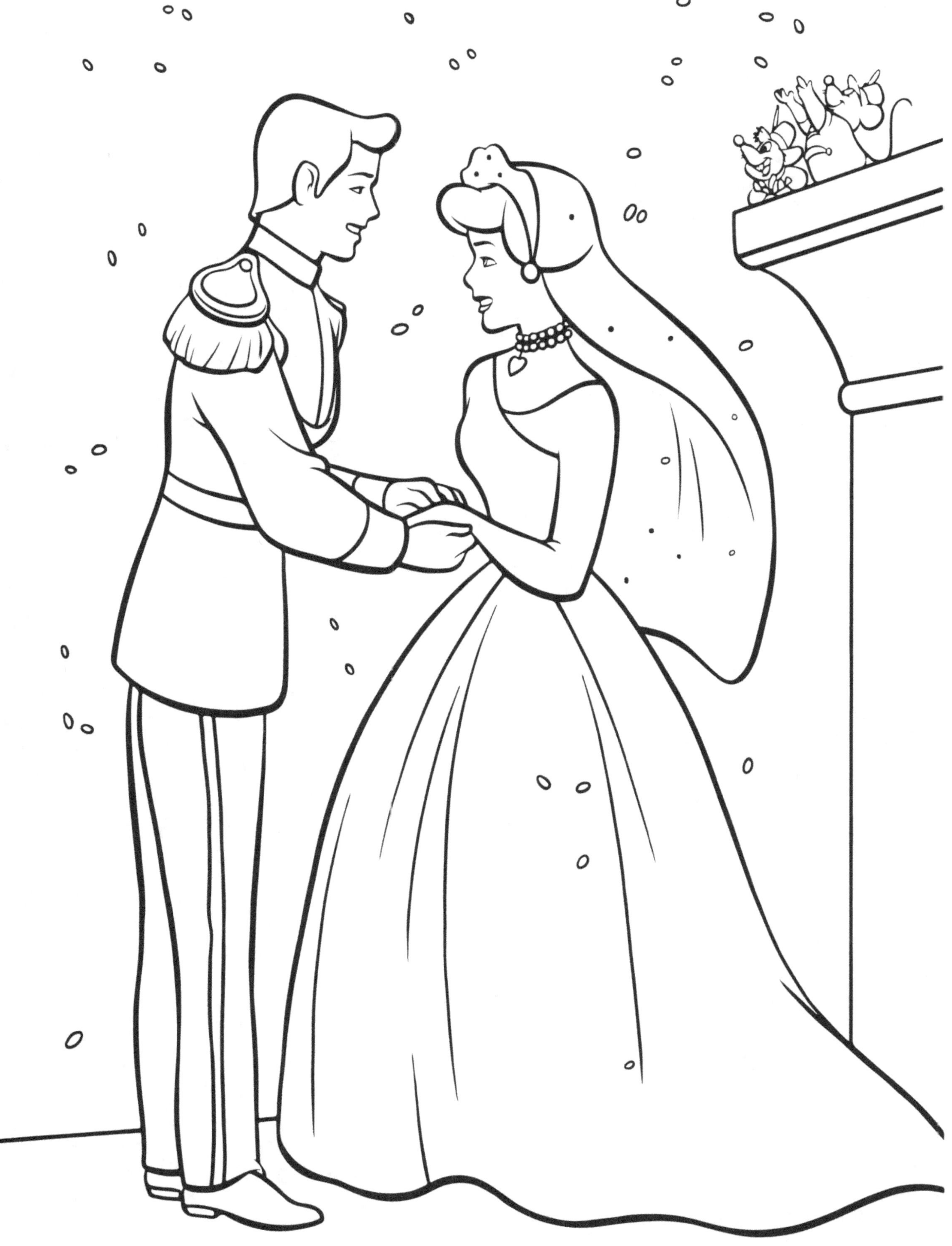

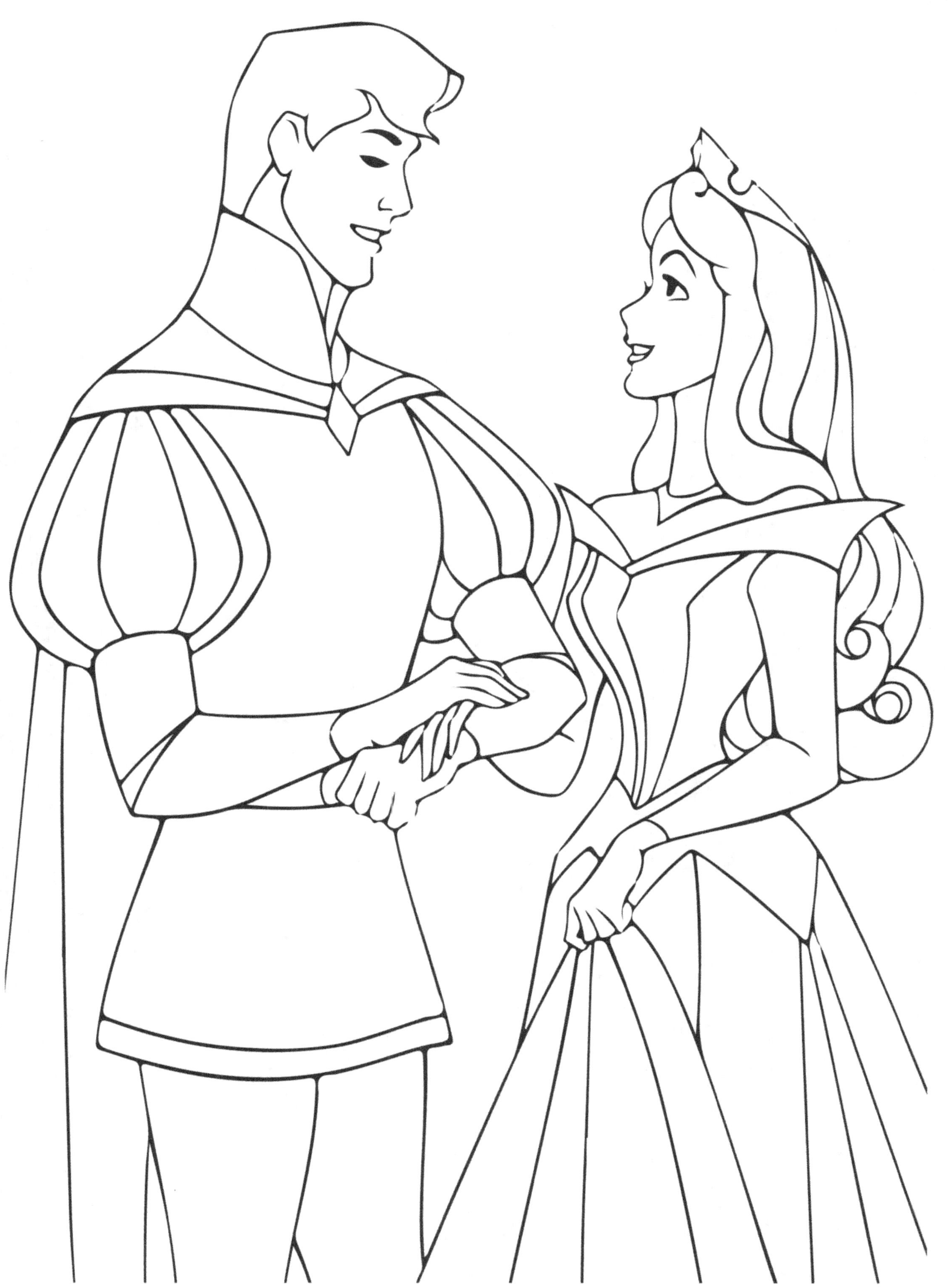

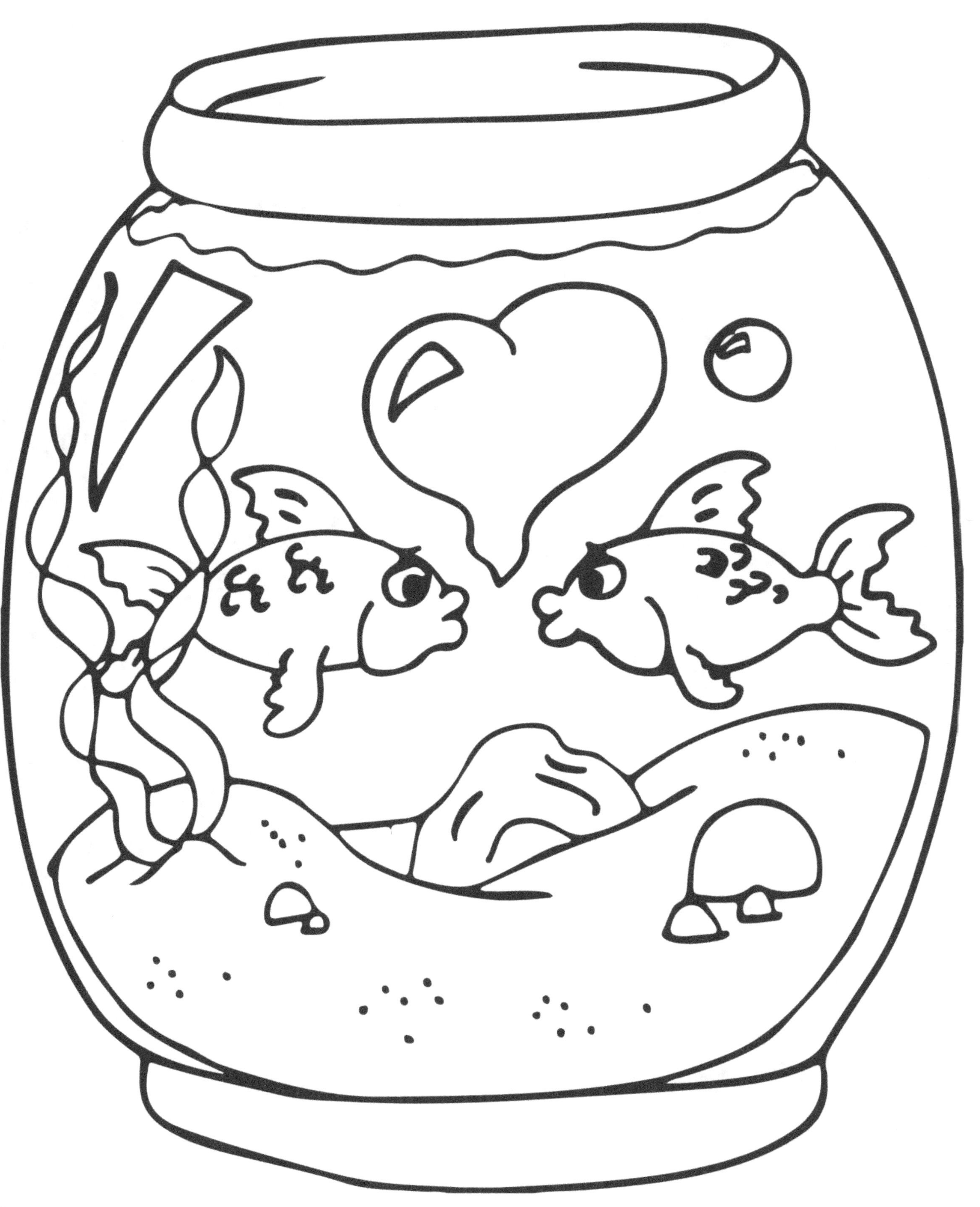

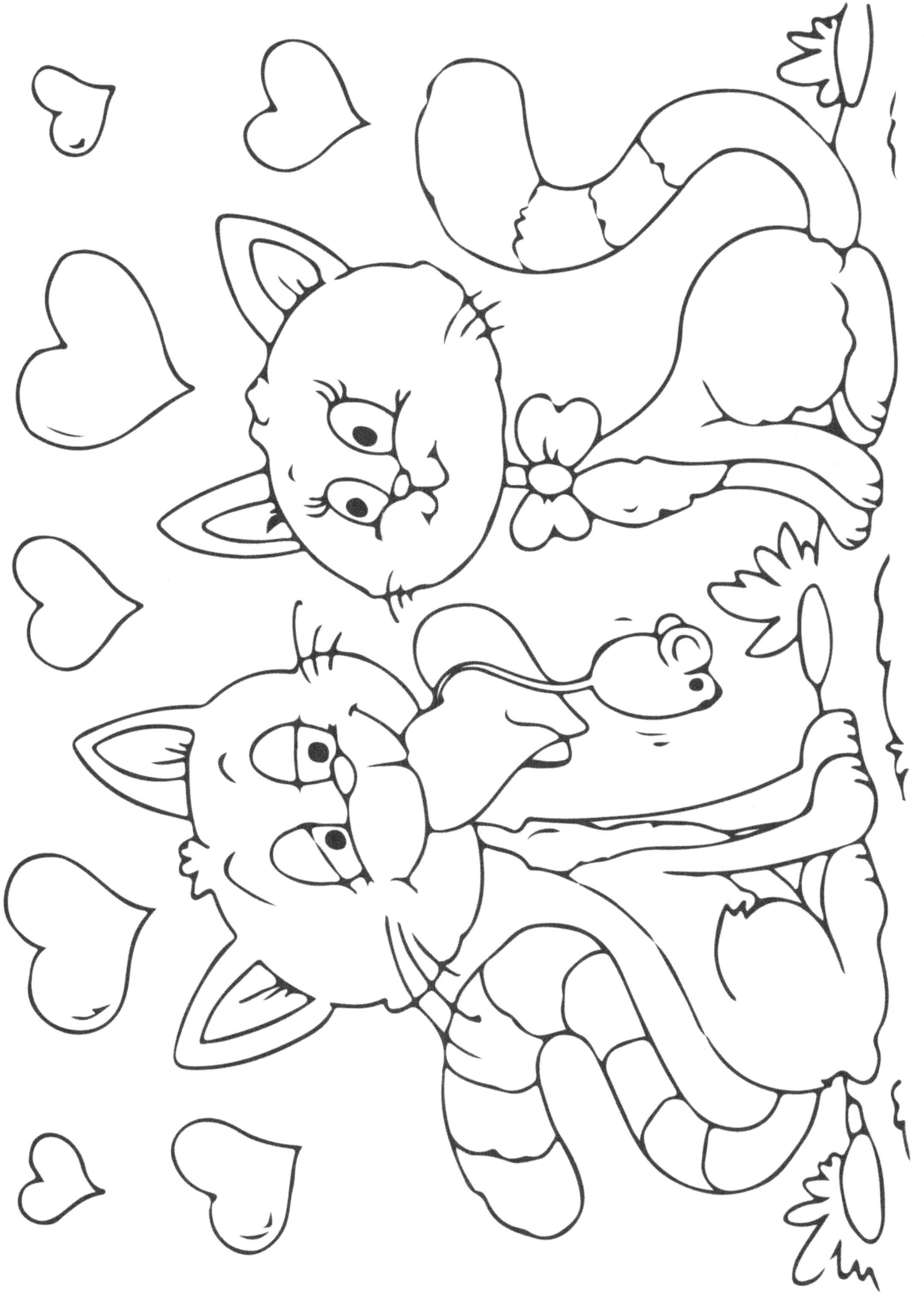

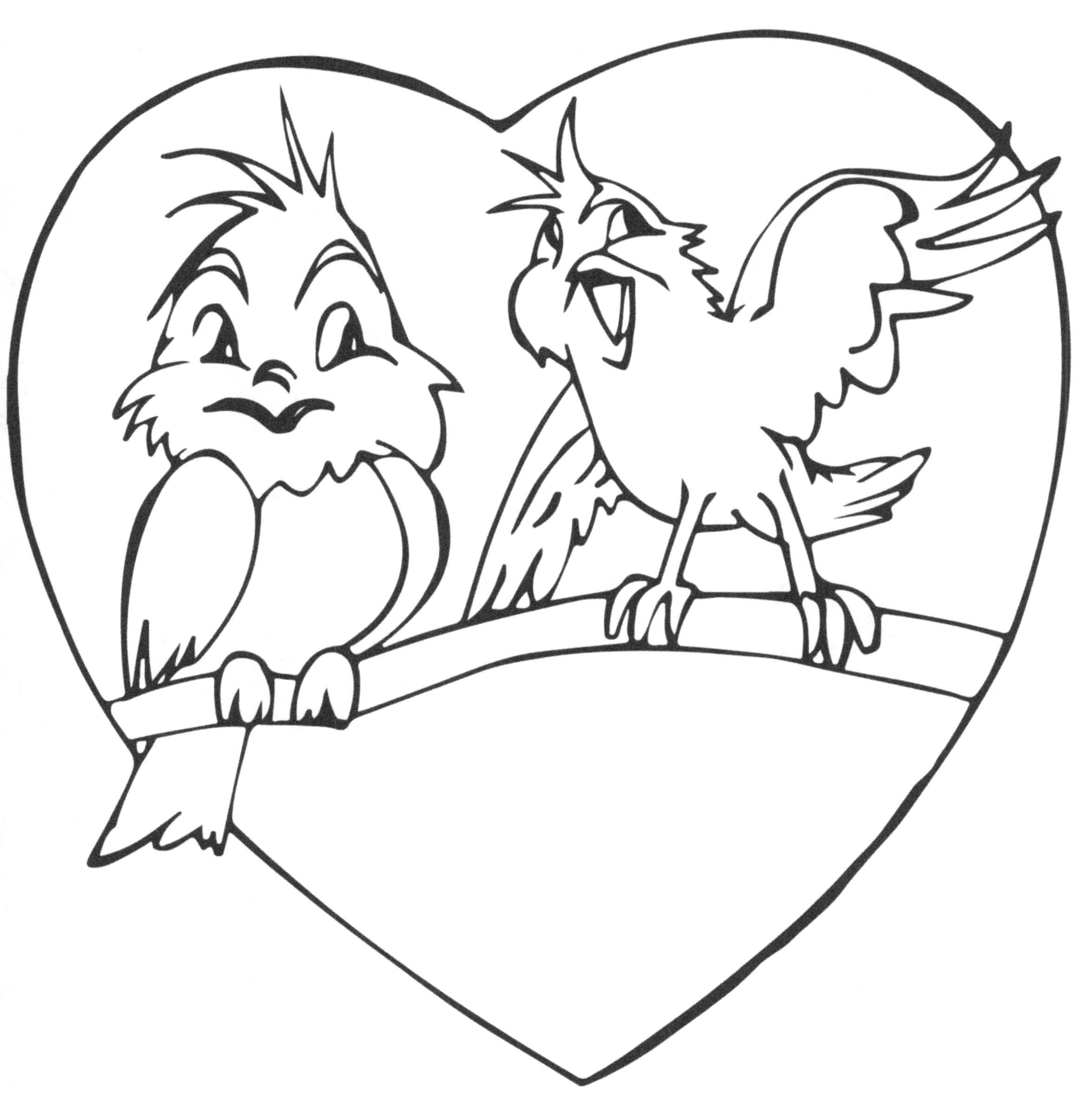

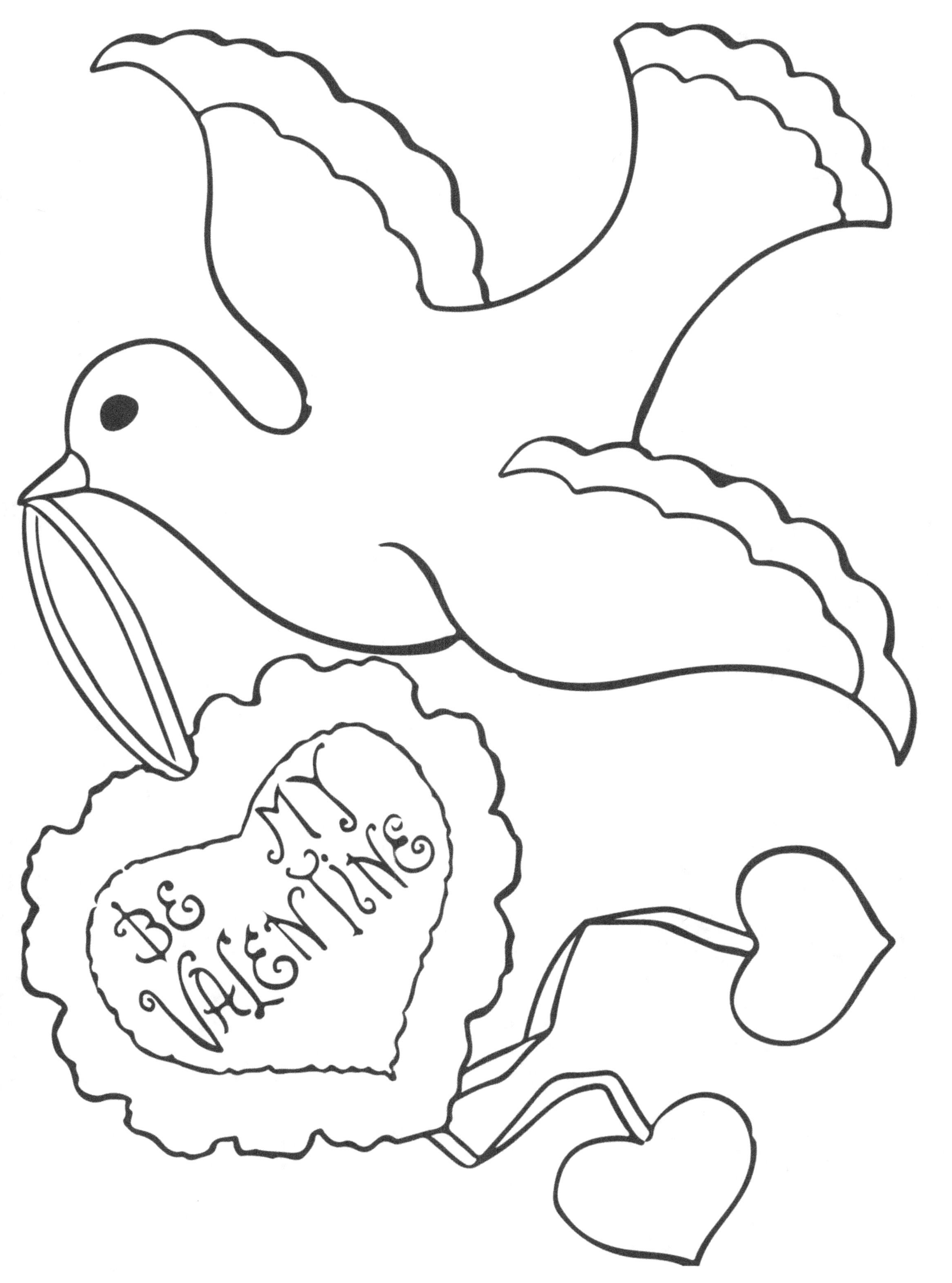
BE MY VALENTINE

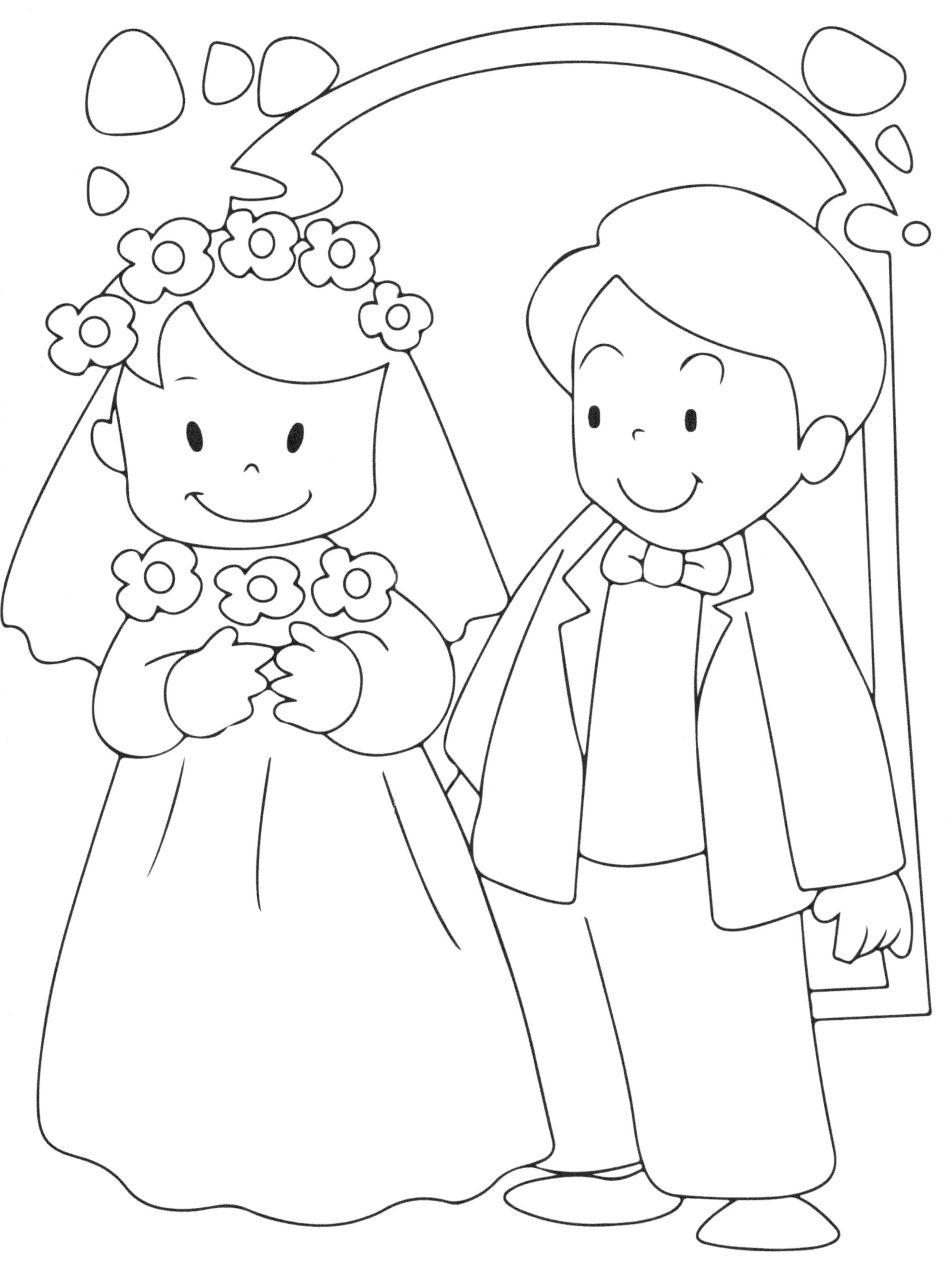

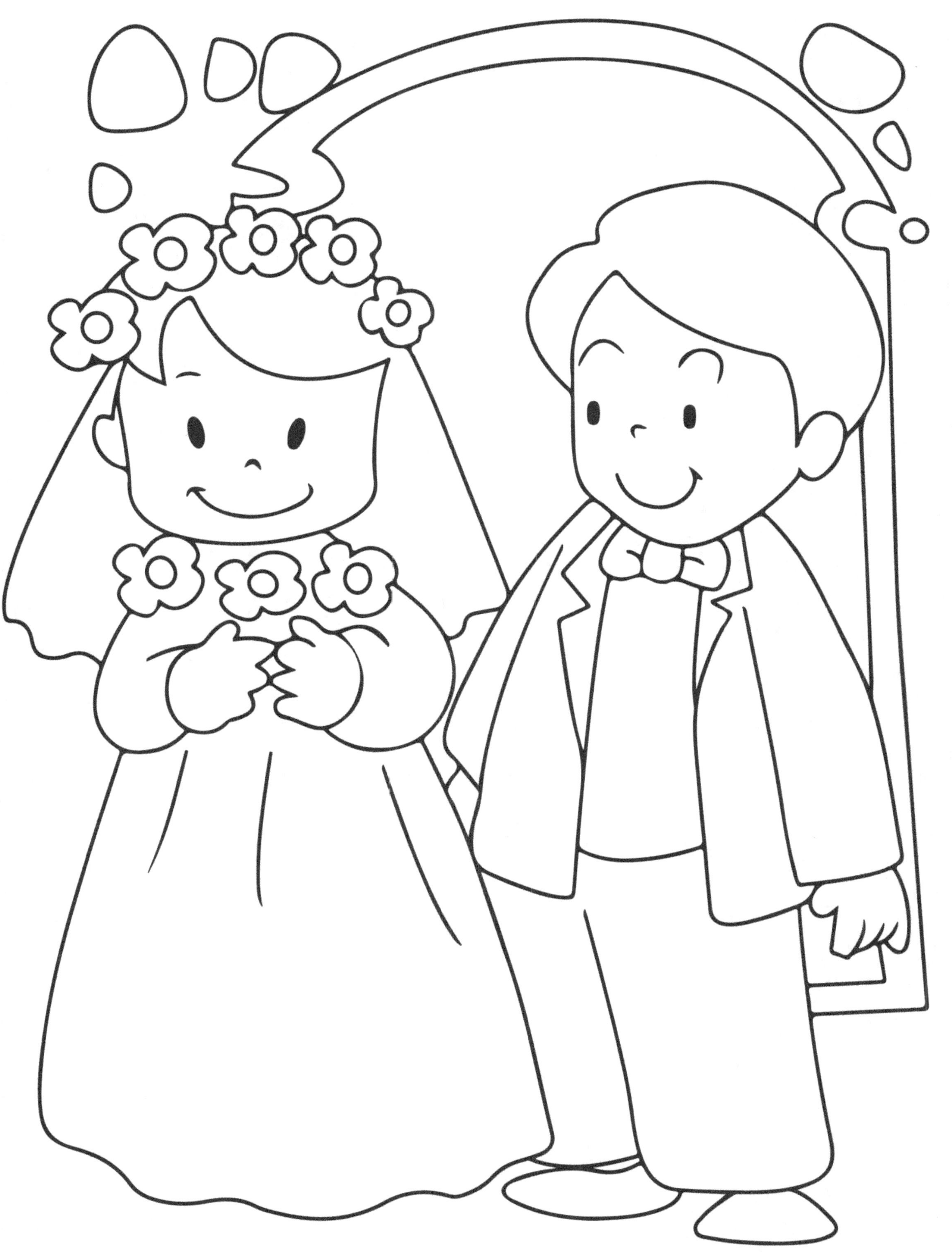

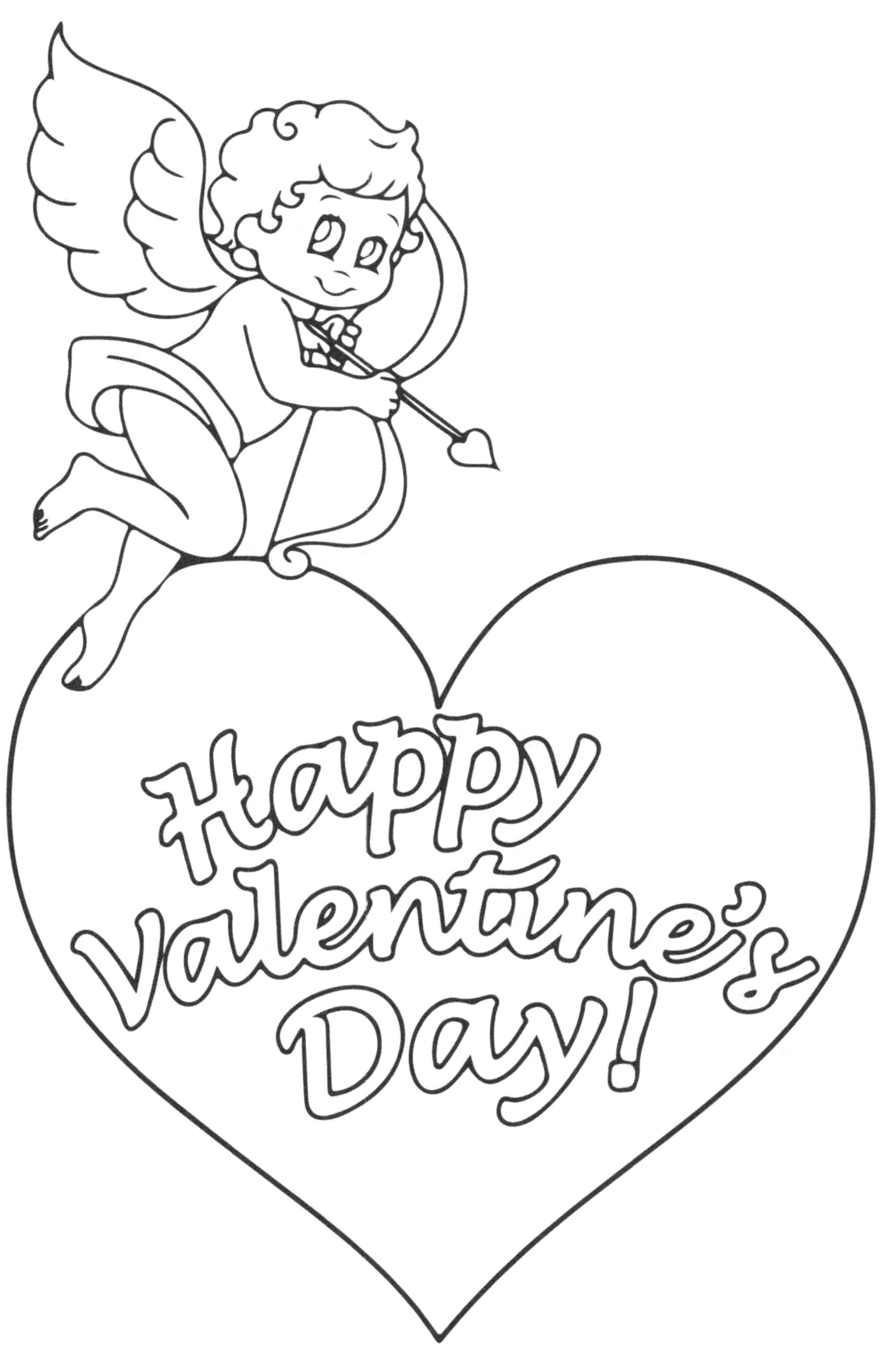

Happy Valentine's Day!

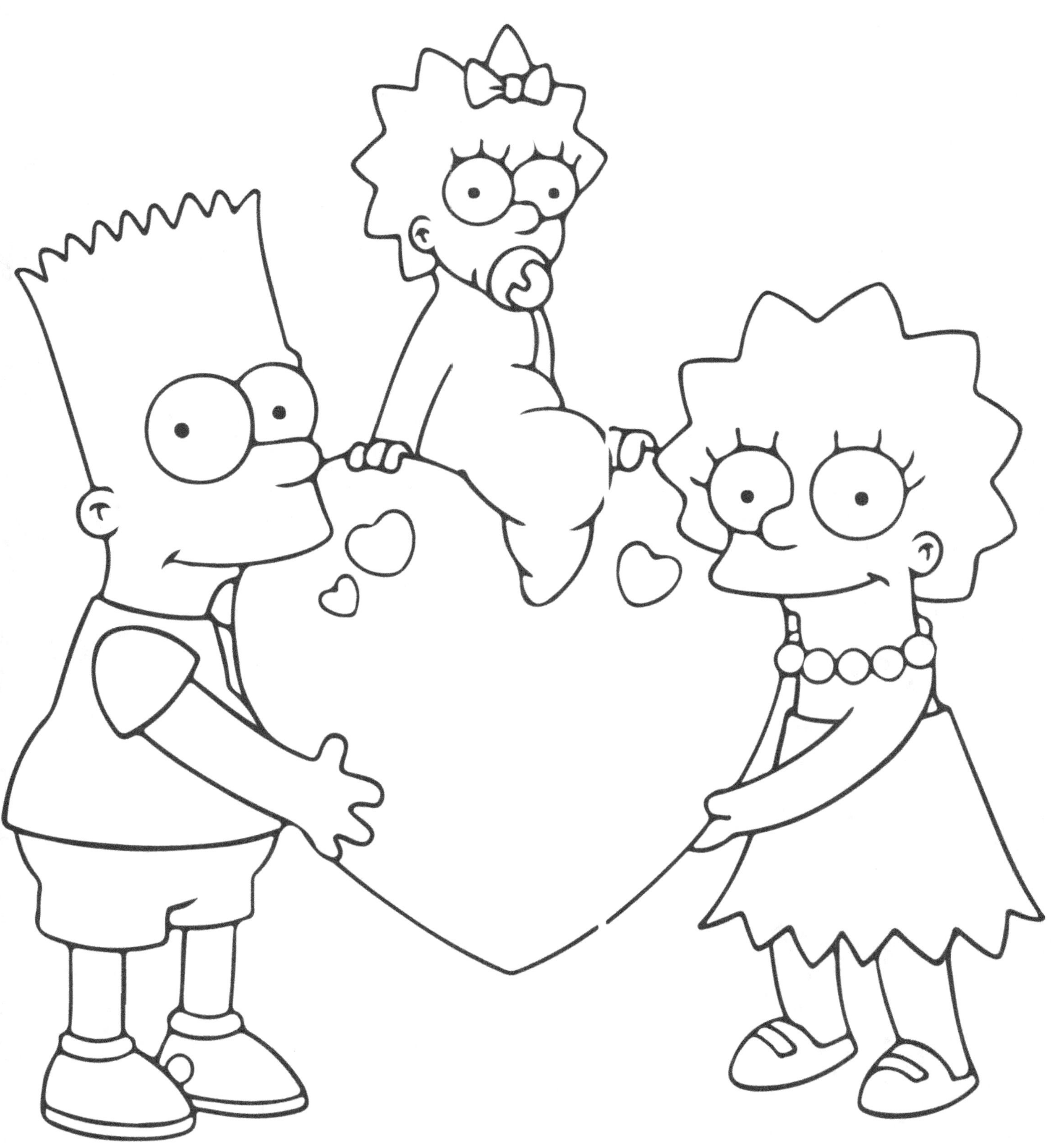

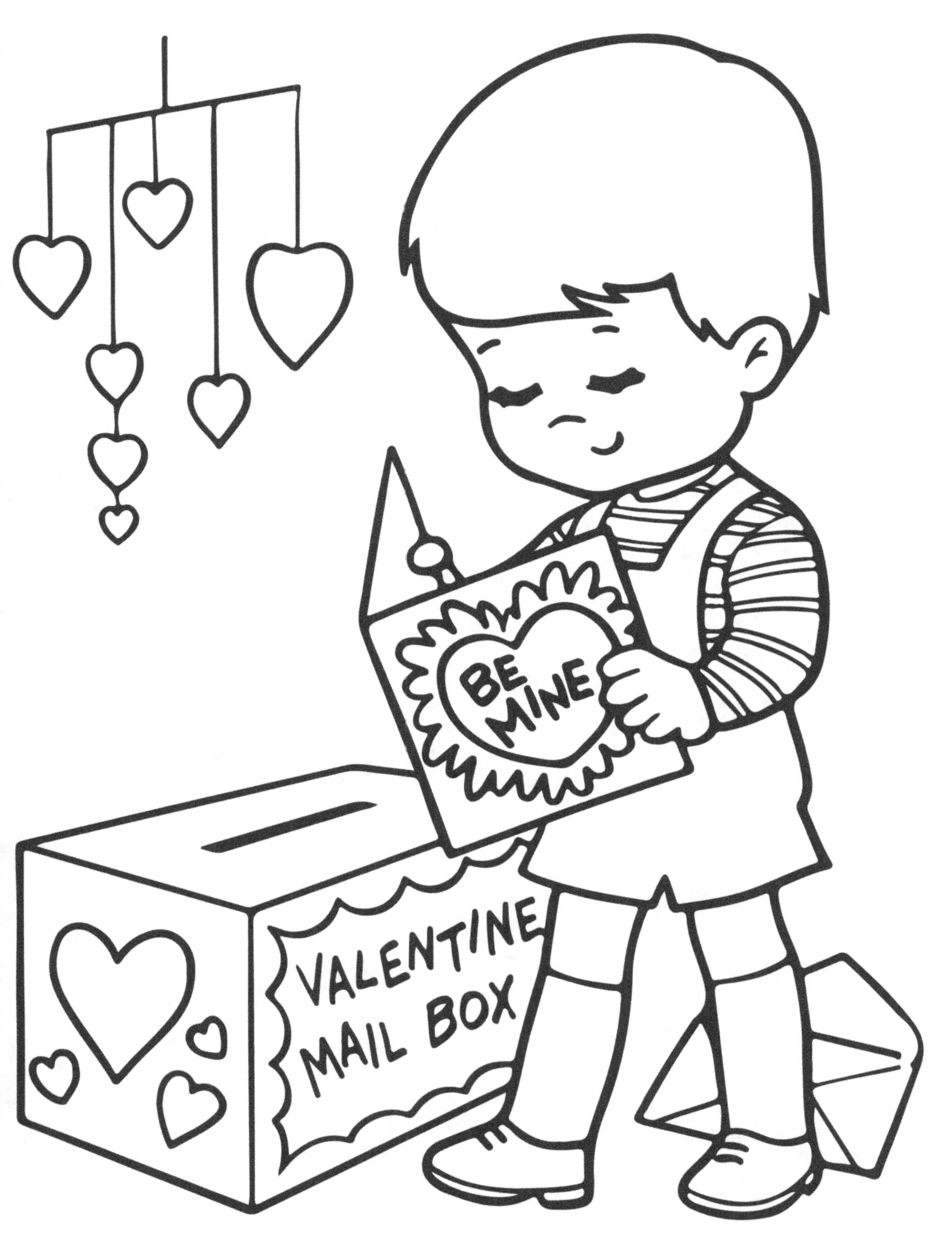

BE MINE
VALENTINE MAIL BOX